YOUR NEW IDENTITY

YOUR NEW IDENTITY

a new creation in Christ

Laura McCluskey

sil Success In Life Publishing

YOUR NEW IDENTITY
ISBN 978-0692291627
Copyright © 2014 by Love Life Church, Inc.

Published by Success In Life Publishing

Published in Spanish with the title of: TU NUEVA IDENTIDAD
© 2007 by Love Life Church. Success in Life Publishing

For information:
Love Life Church, Inc.
8016 W Camelback Rd.
Glendale, Arizona 85303 USA
www.lovelifechurch.com

PRINTED IN THE UNITED STATES OF AMERICA

Dedicated to my husband, Daniel McCluskey, a lover of Jesus and His Word. And the man that the Lord used to teach me and guide me to walk in my new identity in Christ. Thank you for your love.

CONTENTS

1 THE DESIRE OF THE FATHER - A FAMILY

INTRODUCTION

When a child is born into a family, most parents experience the joy and excitement of the paternal nature. Part of this paternal nature includes the desire and the need to impart into this new being three key elements in a particular order. Unconditional love is the first element, shown by providing a safe home and making sure all of the child's needs are met. Then comes the introduction of the family members, including how each person is related to him or her. After this, the parents begin to identify each of the characteristics and features that make this new being someone unique and special. All of this basic information will eventually help establish the identity of this new individual.

Behold what manner of love the Father has bestowed on us, that we should be called children of God! (1 John 3:1)

You are called a child of God when you believe and confess that Jesus Christ is your Lord and Savior. At that moment, you are born again into God's family, and before God, you become a new creation.

As a new creation in Christ, it is important for you to build your identity based on the same principles of the paternal nature. This study is designed to help you realize and know your new identity in Christ, by getting to know your heavenly Father and His unconditional love toward you, the purpose of your life and all that He has designed for you, and your position, rights, and privileges in this great family—the family of God.

Once you have received the revelation of your new identity in Christ, you will be able to be free from feelings of guilt, condemnation, inferiority, inability, inadequacy, and from any other bondages that have hindered you from developing into the person that God predestined you to be.

A NEW CREATION

Let's begin with 2 Corinthians 5:16 and 17:

Therefore, from now on, we regard no one according to the flesh. Even though we have known Christ according to the flesh, yet now we know Him thus no longer. Therefore, if anyone is in Christ, he is a new creation; old things have passed away; behold, all things have become new. (2 Corinthians 5:16,17)

From the previous verses, we can recognize that God not only desires you to know that you are a new being—a new creation—He also desires that what you've known up to this point, about yourself and about Him, stays in the past, without being considered any longer.

Perhaps you consider or know yourself to be a very shy, fearful, or angry person. But who you *are* right now is only the result of your natural life, such as your training and the influence you have received during your whole life according to your surroundings and environment. By receiving and applying God's Word in your life, you will discover that the personality that you have come to know as you, is not necessarily your real personality and therefore can be changed. As a child of God, you now live a spiritual life. A life without barriers or limitations, a life full of freedom and power!

A new creation means a new creature, somebody that has never existed; therefore, somebody that doesn't have a past.

How does this happen? Surely, you have seen yourself in a mirror after being born again and noticed that "you seemed the same." The fact is, you are not! But to get a better understanding of the new creation's unseen characteristics, you have to understand how you were created, and that is what we will be studying next.

A THREE-PART BEING

Humanity was created in the image and likeness of God.

Then God said, "Let Us make man in Our image, according to Our likeness; let them have dominion over the fish of the sea, over the birds of the air, and over the cattle, over all the earth and over every creeping thing that creeps on the earth." (Genesis 1:26)

God is a Triune Being. He is one God, manifested in three different personalities: God the Father, God the Son, and God the Holy Spirit.

The Bible teaches us that we were formed in the image and likeness of God. We were formed as a three-part being: spirit, soul, and body (1 Thessalonians 5:23).

- **You are a spirit.** Your spirit is the part that can have a relationship with God and with the spiritual world.

- **You have a soul.** Your soul consists of your emotions, your will, and your intellect. It is the part of you that allows you to relate or interact in the natural world.

- **You live in a body.** Your body is the house where your spirit lives.

Understanding that you are a spirit is the key to your success as a Christian. It gives you the ability to receive all the benefits and privileges that God prepared for you.

CREATED IN THE IMAGE OF GOD

God had a purpose and a plan when He created man and woman in His own image. What was that purpose?

Then God said, "Let Us make man in Our image, according to Our likeness; let them have dominion over the fish of the sea, over the birds of the air, and over the cattle, over all the earth and over every creeping thing that creeps on the earth." So God created man in His own image; in the image of God He created him; male and female He created them. Then God blessed them, and God said to them, "Be fruitful and multiply; fill the earth and subdue it; have dominion over the fish of the sea, over the birds of the air, and over every living thing that moves on the earth." (Genesis 1:26-28)

God created humanity so that they would have an intimate relationship with Him, but this relationship ought to be developed in a voluntary way. This is why God gave man and woman a free will. They had the ability to choose to be for or against God. They could choose to obey or disobey. This free will was manifested by the tree of the knowledge of good and evil.

And out of the ground the Lord God made every tree grow that is pleasant to the sight and good for food. The tree of life *was* also in the midst of the garden, and the tree of the knowledge of good and evil. (Genesis 2:9)

"But of the tree of the knowledge of good and evil you shall not eat, for in the day that you eat of it you shall surely die." (Genesis 2:17)

Besides free will, God created man and woman in the following manner.

THE ORIGINAL STATE

And the LORD God formed man of the dust of the ground, and breathed into his nostrils the breath of life; and man became a living being. (Genesis 2:7)

Adam and Eve were created in the image of God, with the breath of God. They were alive not only in the natural way that you and I live, but they were also spiritually alive.

In this original state, Adam and Eve experienced their humanity in its perfect condition, which included:

- Perfect communion with God. Being spiritually alive, they had the ability to have face-to-face fellowship with God. They could come to Him without fear, feelings of guilt, condemnation, or inferiority.

- Complete physical health, power and strength, with the ability to live forever.

- Complete mental health. Adam and Eve's souls (intellect, will, and emotions) were in perfect harmony with God, with the ability to imagine, create, and innovate.

- Complete authority and dominion over the earth and all its inhabitants.

- Complete spiritual perception, with the ability to operate beyond the five natural senses.

- Crowned with the glory of God. The glory of God covered all of their being. This is why they did not need to wear clothes.

THE BAD NEWS

Humanity was created to have intimate fellowship with God through a free and voluntary decision. What were man's choices? By choosing to partake of the tree of life, man could have lived united with God forever, by receiving in his human spirit the eternal life of God, and the privilege to become a child of God (Genesis 3:22).

The bad news is that man chose to be independent from God. He decided to disobey God's command by partaking of the tree of the knowledge of good and evil, and as a result, sin entered into the world. This caused spiritual death in humanity.

So when the woman saw that the tree was good for food, that it was pleasant to the eyes, and a tree desirable to make one wise, she took of its fruit and ate. She also gave to her husband with her, and he ate. (Genesis 3:6)

Therefore, just as through one man sin entered the world, and death through sin, and thus death spread to all men, because all sinned. (Romans 5:12)

CONSEQUENCES OF SIN

Once sin entered into humanity, we began to experience the nature of death instead of the nature of life. The nature of death includes, among other consequences:

- Fear. We ended up being fearful of God, knowing that there is not a right relationship between Him and us; fearing punishment and judgment. And through fear came feelings of guilt, condemnation, and shame.

- Slavery. Instead of walking in authority and dominion over the earth, humanity became overpowered by sin and the curse on the earth.

- A new father. Because of sin, the perfect fellowship with God was lost. Now humanity operates under the nature of death, which is of the devil.

SPIRITUAL DEATH

The nature of death is totally opposite of the nature of God. Therefore, by partaking of it, it separates us completely from our Creator. This separation is also known in the Bible as *death* (spiritual death).

For all have sinned and fall short of the glory of God. (Romans 3:23)

For the wages of sin is death. (Romans 6:23)

Sin in humanity is the direct result of the nature of death, also known as *the sin nature.*

And you He made alive, who were dead in trespasses and sins, in which you once walked according to the course of this world, according to the prince of the power of the air, the spirit who now works in the sons of disobedience, among whom also we all once conducted ourselves in the lusts of our flesh, fulfilling the desires of the flesh and of the mind, and were by nature children of wrath, just as the others. (Ephesians 2:1-3)

A MEDIATOR WANTED

In this state of sin, humanity needed a way—a bridge—to be reconciled with God again. Through religion and philosophies, man has tried to create his own bridges to get closer to God. However, the greatest efforts that man can put forth in an attempt to get closer to God are insufficient to reach His presence. If this effort comes from man, then it comes from the sin nature, and therefore, cannot attain fellowship with God, who is Holy and Righteous.

On the other hand, God in His divine state was limited in getting closer to man in a direct way. Because of His Holiness, it is impossible for Him to have communion with sin, or with a sinner.

The answer to restoring the original state of fellowship between God and man was someone that, through his humanity, could identify with man, and having also a nature free of sin, would be able to have communion with God.

Jesus said to him, "I am the way, the truth, and the life. No one comes to the Father except through Me." (John 14:6)

THE GOOD NEWS –JESUS THE PERFECT CANDIDATE

The Son of God was the only one qualified to meet all the required conditions. He came to earth as a man and lived in a perfect way before God, being the perfect sacrifice to restore what had been lost.

Jesus came to the world to be the mediator (bridge) between God and man. This was possible because He had a human nature (the same one that Adam had in the beginning) that was free of sin, which allowed Him to be in communion with the Father.

THE NATURE OF LOVE

Love's nature is to give. In a token of love, Jesus Christ decided to give Himself as a propitiation (sacrifice) for sin (1 John 4:10). What a wonderful demonstration of love!

"Therefore My Father loves Me, because I lay down My life that I may take it again. No one takes it from Me, but I lay it down of Myself. I have power to lay it down, and I have power to take it again. This command I have received from My Father." (John 10:17,18)

This decision was made some time before the problem even existed. The sacrifice of Jesus was a voluntary sacrifice. No one took His life. He gave it with joy, with the faith that He would bring you back to God's family (Hebrews 12:2).

Knowing that you were not redeemed with corruptible things, like silver or gold, from your aimless conduct received by tradition from your fathers, but with the precious blood of Christ, as of a lamb without blemish and without spot. He indeed was foreordained before the foundation of the world, but was manifest in these last times for you. (1 Peter 1:18-20)

This act of love to restore the condition of man did not only involve the work of Jesus—God the Son. The Bible also shows us in John 3:16, that God the Father decided to give up His one and only Son in His love for humanity. Furthermore, in this plan, the Holy Spirit was willing to come and live among us forever. Now, this is love!

SELF QUIZ

What scripture mentions the new creation and what does it say?

What was God's purpose when He created humanity?

How was man created? Describe the three parts.

After Adam and Eve sinned, what were the consequences of sin?

Why do we need a mediator?

2 JESUS THE WAY TO THE FATHER

For there is one God and one Mediator between God and men, the Man Christ Jesus. (1 Timothy 2:5)

Jesus Christ, the second person of Deity, was the only one that could change your nature of death to the nature of life, at the moment that you received Him as your Savior and confessed Him as your Lord. Let's see how this happened.

THE PLAN

In the previous chapter, we studied how Adam was formed to have dominion and authority on the earth. Unfortunately, through a voluntary choice and act, he decided to transfer this legal right to the devil, committing an act of treason—a transgression against God.

And Adam was not deceived, but the woman being deceived, fell into transgression. (1 Timothy 2:14)

As a result, humanity now finds itself under the legal dominion of the devil. But there is hope. God designed a plan to redeem man from the power and the guilt of his own transgression.

THE BLOOD COVENANT

In Him we have redemption through His blood, the forgiveness of sins, according to the riches of His grace. (Ephesians 1:7)

In the plan of redemption, God established from the beginning—before Jesus came to earth—what was known as the Blood Covenant. Through which, each man who partook of it would enter into the promise of perfect redemption from all his sins. God's mercy is amazing!

And according to the law almost all things are purified with blood, and without shedding of blood there is no remission. (Hebrews 9:22)

The Blood Covenant was a perpetual covenant between God Himself and humanity. By promising that in the shedding of the blood of an innocent and spotless animal, He would eventually give an innocent and spotless Redeemer for the forgiveness of sins, through the shedding of the blood of His own Son.

But, why was the sacrifice of His own Son necessary?

GOD IS JUST

He is the Rock, His work is perfect; For all His ways are justice, A God of truth and without injustice; Righteous and upright is He. (Deuteronomy 32:4)

Righteous are You, O LORD, And upright are Your judgments. (Psalms 119:137)

If God were not a just God, He would have punished man and stripped Satan in the very same moment sin entered earth. He is all powerful, but in His justice, He does not take advantage of the weak, including Satan.

Therefore, in order to provide redemption to humanity, He showed His grace and love for man based on perfect justice.

THE DEMAND

Justice demanded man to pay the penalty of his crime. But in this demand, man is incapable of paying even the interest. The payment of his transgression is spiritual death and hell.

For the wages of sin is death. (Romans 6:23)

Man is incapable of redeeming himself of this guilt even with his own death. And in this state, he is condemned to live eternally separated from his Creator.

For the wages of sin is death, but the gift of God is eternal life in Christ Jesus our Lord. (Romans 6:23)

Redemption based on justice establishes that humanity must be freed through a man that can pay the sentence. But all men naturally conceived are under the sin nature. And so, in an act of love, God offered His own Son through incarnation, and as a result, Jesus became the "Lamb of God that takes away the sin of the world."

"Behold! The Lamb of God who takes away the sin of the world!" (John 1:29)

THE LAMB OF GOD

And without controversy great is the mystery of godliness: God was manifested in the flesh, Justified in the Spirit, Seen by angels, Preached among the Gentiles, Believed on in the world, Received up in glory. (1 Timothy 3:16)

The Son has existed forever with the same glory of God. He is the Creator of the Universe and the One that sustains it with His power.

He came to earth taking the form of a man, and once He obtained our redemption through His work on the cross, He rose up and ascended back into heaven, where He now sits at the right hand of God. What a powerful revelation! Now, let's take a brief look at each one of these truths.

THE CREATOR AND HIS PREEXISTENCE

The following are some Scriptures that show Jesus' preexistence:

In the beginning was the Word, and the Word was with God, and the Word was God. He was in the beginning with God. All things were made through Him, and without Him nothing was made that was made. (John 1:1-3)

And now, O Father, glorify Me together with Yourself, with the glory which I had with You before the world was. (John 17:5)

Who being the brightness of His glory and the express image of His person, and upholding all things by the word of His power, when He had by Himself purged our sins, sat down at the right hand of the Majesty on high. (Hebrews 1:3)

THE WORD BECAME FLESH

And the Word became flesh and dwelt among us, and we beheld His glory, the glory as of the only begotten of the Father, full of grace and truth. (John 1:14)

Jesus Christ, the Word of God, became flesh. This means that, in one individual, Deity came in union with humanity. This was the only solution to solve the problem that the nature of death brought to man.

Jesus became flesh by being born of a virgin, being conceived by the Holy Spirit (Luke 1:26-35).

For unto us a Child is born, Unto us a Son is given; And the government will be upon His shoulder. And His name will be called Wonderful, Counselor, Mighty God, Everlasting Father, Prince of Peace. (Isaiah 9:6)

THE MAN JESUS CHRIST

Let this mind be in you which was also in Christ Jesus, who, being in the form of God, did not consider it robbery to be equal with God, but made Himself of no reputation, taking the form of a bondservant, and coming in the likeness of men. And being found in appearance as a man, He humbled Himself and became obedient to the point of death, even the death of the cross. (Philippians 2:5-8)

Therefore, when He came into the world, He said: "Sacrifice and offering You did not desire, But a body You have prepared for Me. (Hebrews 10:5)

Jesus gave up His Deity and came to earth with the same humanity with which Adam had been created (1 Corinthians 15:45). Just as Adam did in the beginning, Jesus partook of a nature free from sin. And just as Adam, He was tempted to sin, with the difference being that He conquered temptation and sin (Hebrews 4:15).

The name of Jesus represents the humanity of the Son, and through this humanity, He not only was able to sympathize with man through a body of flesh and blood, but he could also satisfy the demand of justice for redemption. Let's see how Jesus obtained our redemption.

HE BORE OUR SINS

All we like sheep have gone astray; We have turned, every one, to his own way; And the LORD has laid on Him the iniquity of us all. (Isaiah 53:6)

When we read in the gospels the story of Jesus' crucifixion, we are moved by the cruelty, mistreatment, humiliation, and pain that our Lord suffered unjustly. We are saddened to see the betrayal that turned Him in, as well as the abandonment and loneliness that He suffered from His own people.

This was but only the beginning of His sacrifice. Let's look behind the scenes at the cross, and the way Jesus paid for our sins, since the Bible shows us that it was on the cross where God dealt with Him as our Substitute. God not only dealt with Jesus' body, but also with His soul and His spirit.

But He was wounded for our transgressions, He was bruised for our iniquities. (Isaiah 53:5)

Jesus, who knew no sin, who only did the will of the Father, was now made sin. God put in Him our sin nature. Yes, God took your sins and mine, the sins of all humanity, and put them on Him.

Surely He has borne our griefs and carried our sorrows; Yet we esteemed Him stricken, Smitten by God, and afflicted. (Isaiah 53:4)

Once our sins were put on Jesus, He became sin. This is why the Father turned His back on Him. And it was there that, for the first time, Jesus experienced separation from the Father and spiritual death. He was smitten not only by man, but He was also smitten by God Himself.

And about the ninth hour Jesus cried out with a loud voice, saying, "Eli, Eli, lama sabachthani?" that is, "My God, My God, why have You forsaken Me?" (Matthew 27:46)

On the cross, Jesus died spiritually when the sin nature was put on His Spirit. Once this happened, He then died physically (Matthew 27:50).

But His physical death was not sufficient to obtain our redemption. He also needed to pay the sentence of spiritual death. Where did this sentence get paid?

THE THREE DAYS

"For as Jonah was three days and three nights in the belly of the great fish, so will the Son of Man be three days and three nights in the heart of the earth." (Matthew 12:40)

When Jesus exclaimed on the cross "It is finished" (John 19:30), He was referring to the fulfillment of the Law. As a human, He was able to complete the demands of the Mosaic Law in a perfect way (Romans 8:3,4). But this only fulfilled part of the debt, the natural part. In *Hades* (Greek word for hell), Jesus paid the sentence for spiritual death.

For You will not leave my soul in Hades, Nor will You allow Your Holy One to see corruption. (Acts 2:27)

In Psalms 88 we see a prophetic image of Jesus in *Sheol* (Hebrew word for hell), literally paying for our sins—receiving the punishment in our place.

For my soul is full of troubles, And my life draws near to the grave [*Sheol*] I am counted with those who go down to the pit; I am like a man who has no strength, Adrift among the dead, Like the slain who lie in the grave, Whom You remember no more, And who are cut off from Your hand. You have laid me in the lowest pit, In darkness, in the depths. Your wrath lies heavy upon me, And You have afflicted me with all Your waves. Selah (Psalms 88:3-7)

In these Scriptures we can see that God loved man so much, that He gave His own Son to go to the depths of darkness in our place. And by doing this, God declared His lovingkindness, His faithfulness, His wonders, and His righteousness forever.

MADE ALIVE IN THE SPIRIT

For Christ also suffered once for sins, the just for the unjust, that He might bring us to God, being put to death in the flesh but made alive by the Spirit. (1 Peter 3:18)

Once Jesus completed the demands of justice, by taking upon Himself spiritual death, He was made alive. Jesus was restored with the complete nature of the Father, receiving in His spirit eternal life.

To be made alive in the spirit means that the spirit of Jesus that was alive in the beginning, suffered death on the cross (separation from God), and once He was judged and paid the sentence, He was legally justified in His spirit (1 Timothy 3:16).

When Jesus Christ was made alive, He was born of the Spirit, being the firstborn among the dead.

And He is the head of the body, the church, who is the beginning, the firstborn from the dead, that in all things He may have the preeminence. (Colossians 1:18)

RISEN AGAIN

"Do not be afraid; I am the First and the Last. I am He who lives, and was dead, and behold, I am alive forevermore. Amen. And I have the keys of Hades and of Death." (Revelation 1:17,18)

Jesus Christ, with the life of God in Him, rose amongst the dead as a Conqueror. Not only did He pay the price for our redemption, but He also stripped the devil of the authority that once belonged to Adam.

Now all authority and dominion belong to Him legally. He is Lord!

And Jesus came and spoke to them, saying, "All authority has been given to Me in heaven and on earth." (Matthew 28:18)

He has conquered not only the power of sin, but sin nature and death itself (1 Corinthians 15:55).

"I will ransom them from the power of the grave; I will redeem them from death. O Death, I will be your plagues! O Grave, I will be your destruction! Pity is hidden from My eyes." (Hosea 13:14)

Now redemption and eternal life are available freely to all that believe and confess Jesus Christ as Lord. He is the only way to the Father.

When we receive Jesus Christ as our Lord, we are free of condemnation and judgment. Our Redeemer has reconciled us with the Father! Now we can enter into the holy presence of God without fear (Hebrews 9:12).

And you, being dead in your trespasses and the uncircumcision of your flesh, He has made alive together with Him, having forgiven you all trespasses. (Colossians 2:13)

Jesus Christ obtained our eternal redemption. Through Him we receive not only the forgiveness of sins, but a new nature—the nature of life, the eternal life of God Himself. Thank God for Jesus Christ!

SELF QUIZ

According to 1 Timothy 2:5, how many mediators are there between God and men?

What is the meaning of the Blood Covenant?

What is sin's payment and where does it get paid?

Why is Jesus the only mediator between God and men?

Describe Jesus' work of redemption.

3 REDEEMED IN HIM

In Him we have redemption through His blood, the forgiveness of sins, according to the riches of His grace. (Ephesians 1:7)

The purpose of man's redemption is the same purpose with which he was created: to have communion with the Father. Through the new birth, fellowship between God and man is restored.

The plan of redemption is the way in which God legally delivered man from the nature of death and stripped Satan of his dominion over him.

REDEMPTION

Perhaps you have heard the word redemption and have an idea of what it means. But having an idea on a subject is not enough. In fact, the Bible shows us in Matthew 13:19, that when you hear the Word and you don't understand it, you lose out on receiving the benefits from it.

Sadly, in these days, there are many Christians that don't have a complete understanding of what redemption is. For some, it's something they try to obtain by their own works; for others, it's simply the way to get to heaven. And because of a lack of understanding of all that redemption provides to the believer, many Christians live lives of defeat and survival, instead of experiencing the abundant life that Jesus Christ came to give us, which includes authority, dominion, and prosperity in every area of our lives.

Let's see some of the meanings of the word *redemption*:

- To buy. The purchase of a slave with the purpose of making him free
- To release when the price of rescue has been paid
- To be freed
- To free from debt, oppression, torture, and sin
- To forgive

Before the new birth, we were identified with Adam, who ended up being a slave of Satan, of sin, and of death. We experienced guilt, shame, oppression, and fear of judgment from God. We were slaves, yearning for freedom in our spirit, soul, and body.

By receiving the revelation of what redemption provides for us through Christ, we must now be identified with Him, walking in the freedom of our new nature. Our past no longer exists and now we can come boldly before the Father, to love Him and receive His love, free from condemnation and remorse. We have been redeemed!

ETERNAL LIFE

The new birth does not consist in the conversion of new ideas or beliefs, contrary to the religions of the world. To be born again is a real and supernatural experience.

"And this is eternal life, that they may know You, the only true God, and Jesus Christ whom You have sent." (John 17:3)

The moment you were born again, when you believed and confessed Jesus Christ as your Lord and Savior, your spirit was made alive. Now you are a spiritual being alive before the Father.

From the previous chapters, we can understand that all humans are spiritual beings, either spiritually alive through faith in Jesus Christ (John 20:31), or spiritually dead and separated from the presence of God (Romans 3:23).

"Most assuredly, I say to you, he who hears My word and believes in Him who sent Me has everlasting life, and shall not come into judgment, but has passed from death into life." (John 5:24)

Through the new birth you have passed from death to life! The eternal life that Jesus Christ received when He rose again, has given you life in Him.

When the Bible refers to the spiritual life that comes from God to us, the Greek word *zoe* is used, which pertains to God's quality of life—the same life of God.

And it is the same life of God that you have received in your spirit! When you received the life of God, not only were you forgiven of your sins, but your old nature changed. Now you have the eternal life of God in you, and therefore, you have been redeemed from condemnation and from judgment.

"For God so loved the world that He gave His only begotten Son, that whoever believes in Him should not perish but have everlasting life. "For God did not send His Son into the world to condemn the world, but that the world through Him might be saved. "He who believes in Him is not condemned." (John 3:16-18)

ONE SAME SPIRIT

Through redemption, we have become one with Him. Just as through Adam we became partakers of the nature of death, now, through Christ, we are partakers of the nature of life.

For as in Adam all die, even so in Christ all shall be made alive. (1 Corinthians 15:22)

By receiving the life of God, we become partakers of His own nature.

By which have been given to us exceedingly great and precious promises, that through these you may be partakers of the divine nature. (2 Peter 1:4)

How wonderful it is to know that the same Spirit of God not only dwells in us, but has also become one with our spirit.

That they all may be one, as You, Father, are in Me, and I in You; that they also may be one in Us, that the world may believe that You sent Me. I in them, and You in Me; that they may be made perfect in one, and that the world may know that You have sent Me, and have loved them as You have loved Me. (John 17:21,23)

The desire of the Father has become a reality in Jesus Christ. Through Him, we can be in complete unity with the Father, being loved by Him with the same love with which He loved Jesus. We are children of God.

RIGHTEOUSNESS

Being justified freely by His grace through the redemption that is in Christ Jesus. (Romans 3:24)

Righteousness is the foundation of God's grace and love. The Word shows us that the Father has loved man with an everlasting love (Jeremiah 31:3). But in spite of His love, He couldn't forgive and forget man's sins, until man could become righteous before Him. Unless man is righteous, he cannot have communion with God on equal terms, and therefore, he cannot enjoy His love.

Redemption provides righteousness. This righteousness transforms a sinner into a righteous person.

Who was delivered up because of our offenses, and was raised because of our justification. (Romans 4:25)

When Jesus Christ rose from the dead, we were declared justified—legally righteous before God. And being righteous, we can have perfect communion with the Father.

By receiving the nature of God, we receive His righteousness, becoming as righteous as He is.

We can define righteousness as the ability to stand in the presence of God without sin, guilt, or inferiority.

For He made Him who knew no sin to be sin for us, that we might become the righteousness of God in Him. (2 Corinthians 5:21)

In Christ, we are made the righteousness of God. He was made sin for us, so we could be made His righteousness.

Who Himself bore our sins in His own body on the tree, that we, having died to sins, might live for righteousness–by whose stripes you were healed. (1 Peter 2:24)

The righteousness we have received doesn't just come with the benefit of going to heaven at a later point in your life; it also comes with a present benefit, which is a freedom that is meant to be enjoyed now!

You may think, "How is this possible since I am conscious that I am a sinner?"

But if you have been born again, then you *were* a sinner. Now you are the righteousness of God in Christ. Now you should be conscious of that.

Your righteousness is not based on your own works. Know that righteousness, as well as grace, are gifts from God. In other words, it is something you have received freely through redemption.

For if by the one man's offense death reigned through the one, much more those who receive abundance of grace and of the gift of righteousness will reign in life through the One, Jesus Christ. (Romans 5:17)

God did His part when He redeemed you. Your part now is to believe and confess what the Father says about you in His Word. And He says that you have been made righteous, that you are an heir of eternal life, and a partaker of His divine nature.

FREE FROM SIN

For the law of the Spirit of life in Christ Jesus has made me free from the law of sin and death. (Romans 8:2)

Redemption has freed you from the slavery of sin. In Christ, we no longer live under the law of sin and death. Our nature has changed, so now we partake of God's pure and holy nature; we partake of His righteousness.

How does redemption free us from sin? First and foremost, you need to remember that the problem that God solved through redemption was not the *actions* of sin that man had committed, but the *nature* that produces these actions, the nature of death, whose fruit is sin.

Therefore, to free man of these sinful acts, it was necessary to change his *nature*.

Religion has told us that in order to stop committing sin, we need laws or moral rules. However, these do not have the power to change the nature of man, only the new birth frees us from the slavery of sin.

When a person has not been born again, this person not only is a sinner, but is sin himself. His nature is sin, and regardless of his efforts, he will not stop sinning until he is freed from that nature.

As a new creation, in unity with the Spirit of God, you no longer have the nature of death, which means that you no longer are under the slavery of sin. Your new nature cannot produce sin.

Whoever has been born of God does not sin, for His seed remains in him; and he cannot sin, because he has been born of God. (1 John 3:9)

The Word shows us that since we've been born of the Spirit, and since our spirit is in complete unity with the Spirit of the Father, then our spirit—our true being—cannot sin. It is impossible, because God is Holy, and He won't have anything to do with sin.

Let's read the previous verse again, this time with the understanding of the nature of life. Also keep in mind that the word "do" used in "does not sin," is the Greek word *poieo*, which originally means: *to produce through the nature, from the inward*, and *to create*. But it is sometimes just translated to English as *to practice, to do*, or *to commit*.

Whoever has been born of God *does* not [*does not produce by nature*] sin, for His seed remains in him; and he cannot sin, because he has been born of God. (1 John 3:9)

Let's see one more example where the word *poieo* is used in reference to sin, this time translated as "commit":

Jesus answered them, "Most assuredly, I say to you, whoever *commits* [*by nature*] sin is a slave of sin." (John 8:34)

These verses, among many others, allow us to understand that when a person is born again, he no longer sins through his nature. But, if a person sins because of his nature, then he is a slave to sin, and therefore has not been born of God.

And having been set free from sin, you became slaves of righteousness. (Romans 6:18)

Through redemption in Christ, the nature of sin no longer has authority over us. We have been set free.

For sin shall not have dominion over you, for you are not under law but under grace. (Romans 6:14)

However, being free, we can *voluntarily* submit ourselves to sin, not in our nature or spirit, but by our own decision through our body and mind. This is what the next verse calls "serving sin."

Knowing this, that our old man is crucified with *him*, that the body of sin might be destroyed, that henceforth we should not serve sin. (Romans 6:6 KJV)

There is a difference between being a *slave* to sin and *serving* sin by our own choice. For now, we have only focused on the redemption from the slavery of sin. In the next chapter, we will study how to be restored after we have served sin by a voluntarily choice.

DOMINION OVER SATAN

He has delivered us from the power of darkness and conveyed us into the kingdom of the Son of His love. (Colossians 1:13)

Before becoming new creations, we were under the slavery of Satan. He legally had complete dominion over us. To rob us, destroy us, and ultimately kill us (John 10:10).

Now as children of God, we have been delivered from Satan's authority. We have been translated into the kingdom of His beloved Son! And not only that, we now have power and authority over Satan and every demonic power.

"And these signs will follow those who believe: In My name they will cast out demons; they will speak with new tongues; they will take up serpents; and if they drink anything deadly, it will by no means hurt them; they will lay hands on the sick, and they will recover." (Mark 16:17,18)

In the name of Jesus, we have authority not only over demonic powers, but over every situation that may present itself against us, such as sickness, oppression, fear, etc.

You are of God, little children, and have overcome them, because He who is in you is greater than he who is in the world. (1 John 4:4)

Being in unity with the Spirit of God in us, we can boldly say "Greater is He that is in me, than he who is in the world!" Now, we can fulfill the purpose with which God created us, to have dominion over the earth. Following the example of Jesus, we can take authority not only over the spiritual powers of darkness, but also over every natural situation that has to submit to the authority of Jesus Christ (Genesis 1:28).

FREE FROM THE CURSE

Christ has redeemed us from the curse of the law, having become a curse for us (for it is written, "Cursed is everyone who hangs on a tree") (Galatians 3:13)

The curse entered earth when Adam turned over his authority to Satan. From that moment, death has reigned in it. Romans 8:20-22 shows us that because of sin, all creation is subject to corruption and is in bondage to death and destruction. This is why we live in a world of danger, where natural disasters, violence, plagues, and pestilence seem to be uncontrollable.

In Deuteronomy 28:15-68, the Word shows us a list of what the curse involves. Let's see a brief summary of the curse in the following categories:

- Failure
- Poverty
- Sickness
- Pain
- Slavery
- Defeat
- Humiliation
- Robbery and Loss
- Fear
- Oppression and Depression
- Plagues and Pestilence
- Dissatisfaction
- Sadness
- Danger
- Death
- Disaster, etc.

Thank God that in Christ, we have been redeemed from the curse and its effects! As you can see, it is important to know from what we have been delivered, otherwise, we will live life suffering the consequences of the curse, even when it no longer has power and authority over us.

Blessed be the God and Father of our Lord Jesus Christ, who has blessed us with every spiritual blessing in the heavenly places in Christ. (Ephesians 1:3)

We have been blessed by the Father; therefore, the curse no longer has power over our lives. Know that if you've been blessed, there is no curse big enough that can revoke your blessing.

He has blessed, and I cannot reverse it. (Numbers 23:20)

SALVATION

Remember that you are a born-again spirit; you are a new creation. And as a new creation, you have been redeemed with a complete salvation.

Now may the God of peace Himself sanctify you completely; and may your whole spirit, soul, and body be preserved blameless at the coming of our Lord Jesus Christ. (1 Thessalonians 5:23)

Salvation not only includes eternal life after you die physically, it also includes the restoration of your soul and body here on earth so you can live in the fullness of life that the Father predestined for you.

The words for salvation in Greek are *sorteria* and *sozo*, and include among their meanings: *to be saved from danger, from suffering or from the enemy; to be rescued, delivered; health and healing; restoration, to be complete; security and preservation.*

Do you realize the salvation that you have received in Jesus Christ includes spiritual, physical, and mental restoration?

Much more then, having now been justified by His blood, we shall be saved from wrath through Him. For if when we were enemies we were reconciled to God through the death of His Son, much more, having been reconciled, we shall be saved by His life. (Romans 5:9,10)

We have been redeemed, justified, and made children of God. We are new creations with the same authority and power as Jesus Christ. We are partakers of the same nature and fellowship with the Father. We have been delivered from the slavery of sin, from death, and from Satan. We have been delivered from judgment and condemnation, from guilt and fear. We have been saved through our Lord and Savior Jesus Christ!

For God did not appoint us to wrath, but to obtain salvation through our Lord Jesus Christ. (1 Thessalonians 5:9)

This is the true gospel, the good news of great joy! But even so, you may ask, "If I have been redeemed, and I am a child of God, why am I not enjoying this freedom?"

As we saw at the beginning of this lesson, because of a lack of knowledge, ignorance robs you from receiving the benefits of redemption. Once you know your rights and privileges in Christ, it is your responsibility to believe them and receive them by faith—meditating and confessing these beautiful promises that you have learned through the Word of God.

In the following chapters you will learn more Biblical principles that will show you how to appropriate and put to work the promises that the Father has given you as His child.

SELF QUIZ

What does the word redemption mean?

List seven benefits we obtain through redemption.

4 KNOWING THE FATHER

For this reason I bow my knees to the Father of our Lord Jesus Christ, from whom the whole family in heaven and earth is named. (Ephesians 3:14,15)

As you can see, Christianity is not a religion; it is a family relationship that consists of the Father and His children.

Christianity is based on fellowship—on a family relationship between Deity and humanity, God and man. It does not consist of a series of doctrines. Doctrines have only been the result of its teaching. Neither does it consist of laws or moral rules. However, the best moral rules have been the result of its practice. Christianity is not theology, but the reality of the union between the Father and His children. This is what differentiates us from any other religion.

THE STARTING POINT

In the previous lessons, we have been amazed in learning about the love that God the Father has for us, which was manifested in the way He created man, as well as in the way He restored the access for man's fellowship with Him which had been lost once man sinned against Him.

By now, we know that through Jesus Christ, we are saved, we have been redeemed, our sins have been erased, and we are children of God. This is life-transforming, powerful information, and yet, many Christians live today knowing these truths only in their minds, without making them a reality in their lives. Why is this?

To be able to experience the Father's fellowship and all the benefits and privileges that belong to you as His child, you must first have knowledge of it. But once you have obtained this knowledge, it is your responsibility to believe it and put it into practice.

You could, from now on, continue your life the same way you have always lived it. Even with the knowledge you have gained about your eternal life, if there is no application of it, you will not experience its benefits. Believe me, this type of life, even with great eternal hope, will be full of dissatisfaction and frustration.

On the other hand, by using the knowledge of your new nature, and all that is available for you through it, you can begin the best adventure of your life. You can have a life full of freedom and prosperity, enjoying fellowship with your heavenly Father, and using all the resources that He has given to you. You can live a blessed life and be a blessing to others.

I believe the latter is what you desire. It is why you have this book in your hands, isn't it? Let's see then how to develop your fellowship with the Father.

OUR IMAGE OF THE FATHER

Our understanding is based on definitions. In your life, all of your actions and reactions are performed according to the definition you have regarding a given topic or word. Because of that, in your new life in Christ, it is very important that you make sure that the definitions, ideas, or images that you may have about a certain subject, line up with the same definitions that the Father uses in His Word.

Frequently, we base our concept or image of our heavenly Father on the image we may have concerning our earthly father. This influences our fellowship and closeness to Him.

Therefore, from now on, we regard no one according to the flesh. Even though we have known Christ according to the flesh, yet now we know Him thus no longer. (2 Corinthians 5:16)

From the previous verse, we can see that as a new creation, not only are we to change the image that we have about ourselves, but also, we have to leave in the past all ideas, concepts, and images that we may have had regarding God. This is because what we previously knew about Him was in the flesh and in our natural life; therefore, it is not valid now in our new spiritual life.

But the natural man does not receive the things of the Spirit of God, for they are foolishness to him; nor can he know them, because they are spiritually discerned. (1 Corinthians 2:14)

Unfortunately, the bad experiences that we may have had with a father figure in our lives have formed in us wrong feelings or misconceptions, which we will unconsciously use to relate to our heavenly Father, unless they are identified and corrected through the Word.

THE TRUE IMAGE

In the following chart, we will see some examples of negative experiences we might have had with an earthly father that might cloud our image of our heavenly Father.

Seeing the comparison between our preconceived ideas and the Father's true image can help us change our view and beliefs about our heavenly Father, providing us boldness and freedom to come before Him.

Our Earthly Father	Our Heavenly Father
Absence. Many people grew up with the absence of a father or father figure. As a result, this could have created the idea that God can only be God to them, but not a Father.	For He Himself has said, I will never leave you nor forsake you. (Hebrews 13:5) "I am with you always, even to the end of the age. Amen." (Matthew 28:20)
Indifference. Perhaps the father was an indifferent person or a very busy one, unable to dedicate time to his children. This may create the feeling that God is indifferent or too busy to deal with their issues.	Casting all your care upon Him, for He cares for you. (1 Peter 5:7) Be anxious for nothing, but in everything by prayer and supplication, with thanksgiving, let your requests be made known to God. (Philippians 4:6)
Disapproval. Others have grown up with a lack of affection, a lack of their parents' acceptance, or a lack of approval or recognition that most children need from their parents. As a result, they may have a feeling of disapproval before the heavenly Father.	The LORD your God in your midst, The Mighty One, will save; He will rejoice over you with gladness, He will quiet *you* with His love, He will rejoice over you with singing. (Zephaniah 3:17) Having predestined us to adoption as sons by Jesus Christ to Himself, according to the good pleasure of His will ... by which He has made us accepted in the Beloved. (Ephesians 1:5,6)
Demanding. Some fathers, while trying to discipline, used aggressive methods, demanding results out of their children's reach, or harming their development as people. This may have caused fear or a lack of trust to the Father's commandments in His Word.	For this commandment which I command you today *is* not *too* mysterious for you, nor *is* it far off. (Deuteronomy 30:11) These things I have spoken to you, that My joy may remain in you, and *that* your joy may be full. (John 15:11)

Poverty. Some children experience only poverty and lack, either because their father, no matter how hard he tried, couldn't supply all of their needs, or simply because of negligence and ignorance. Either way, these people may grow up with the mindset that the heavenly Father doesn't want to, or He won't, provide for their natural needs.	The LORD is my shepherd; I shall not want. (Psalm 23:1) Beloved, I pray that you may prosper in all things and be in health, just as your soul prospers. (3 John 2) And you shall remember the LORD your God, for it is He who gives you power to get wealth, that He may establish His covenant which He swore to your fathers, as it is this day. (Deuteronomy 8:18)
Abuse. In some cases, the father mistreated or abused his children in a physical, verbal, or even sexual way. This may cause fear and a lack of trust toward the heavenly Father, and sometimes even anger, bitterness, and resentment toward Him.	So he shepherded them according to the integrity of his heart, And guided them by the skillfulness of his hands. (Psalm 78:72) I have seen his ways, and will heal him; I will also lead him, And restore comforts to him And to his mourners. "I create the fruit of the lips: Peace, peace to him who is far off and to him who is near," Says the LORD, "And I will heal him." (Isaiah 57:18,19)
Rejection. Sometimes, children are the result of an unwanted pregnancy. As a consequence, they may grow up with low self-esteem, and with the idea that they are just an accident, without purpose or destiny.	My frame was not hidden from You, When I was made in secret, And skillfully wrought in the lowest parts of the earth. Your eyes saw my substance, being yet unformed. And in Your book they all were written, The days fashioned for me, When as yet there were none of them. (Psalm 139:15-16) Thus says the LORD who made you and formed you from the womb, who will help you: 'Fear not ... My servant ... whom I have chosen. (Isaiah 44:2)

How wonderful it is to know that our heavenly Father loves us and desires nothing but our well-being and prosperity! With this brief information about His character, there is no doubt that you are ready to leave the things of the past in the past, and that you are now ready to allow your heavenly Father to show you the fullness of His love.

That Christ may dwell in your hearts through faith; that you, being rooted and grounded in love, may be able ... to know the love of Christ which passes knowledge; that you may be filled with all the fullness of God. (Ephesians 3:17-19)

CALLED TO BE A SON

But as many as received Him, to them He gave the right to become children of God, to those who believe in His name. (John 1:12)

From the beginning, God's desire has been to be a Father to us. He has longed for you and me to become His children, and to be a part of His family.

"I will be a Father to you, And you shall be My sons and daughters, Says the LORD Almighty." (2 Corinthians 6:18)

But did He not make them one, Having a remnant of the Spirit? And why one? He seeks godly offspring. (Malachi 2:15)

God is not looking for more servants. He has a multitude of angels at His service. We notice this in the parable of the prodigal son that Jesus told.

And he arose and came to his father. But when he was still a great way off, his father saw him and had compassion, and ran and fell on his neck and kissed him. And the son said to him, 'Father, I have sinned against heaven and in your sight, and am no longer worthy to be called your son.'

But the father said to his servants, 'Bring out the best robe and put it on him, and put a ring on his hand and sandals on his feet. And bring the fatted calf here and kill it, and let us eat and be merry'. (Luke 15:20-23)

It is evident in this story that, although the father was offered another servant, his desire was to regain the son he had lost. Notice also, as the story continues, how the oldest son didn't have the attitude or identity of a son either, but of a servant. This attitude kept him from receiving benefits and privileges that he should have enjoyed as a son and heir of his father.

Now his older son was in the field. And as he came and drew near to the house, he heard music and dancing. So he called one of the servants and asked what these things meant. And he said to him, 'Your brother has come, and because he has received him safe and sound, your father has killed the fatted calf.' "But he was angry and would not go in. Therefore his father came out and pleaded with him. So he answered and said to his father, 'Lo, these many years I have been serving you; I never transgressed your commandment at any time; and yet you never gave me a young goat, that I might make merry with my friends. But as soon as this son of yours came, who has devoured your livelihood with harlots, you killed the fatted calf for him.' And he said to him, 'Son, you are always with me, and all that I have is yours'. (Luke 15:25-31)

FELLOWSHIP WITH THE FATHER

Do you realize how important it is to know God as your Father? Your relationship with Him must be based on this truth.

Many times, because of a lack of identity as His children, it is easier for us to relate to Him as God, Lord, Almighty, etc. And there's nothing wrong with these terms when they're used in the proper context, such as worship.

But, when it has to do with daily fellowship, our Father shows us in His Word the way we should communicate toward Him, encouraging us to call Him "Father," or even "Daddy," according to the English translations of the Hebrew word "Abba."

And because you are sons, God has sent forth the Spirit of His Son into your hearts, crying out, "Abba, Father!" (Galatians 4:6)

The Bible shows us clearly that our prayer or communication to God, when it has to do with petitions or reliance, must be directed to the Father, since one of the meanings and functions of a father is to provide and protect. As new creations, we pray to the Father in the name of Jesus.

This prayer or communication toward your heavenly Father does not require eloquent or religious words. Talk to Him the same way you would talk to your dad or your closest friend. And do not worry if you feel like "It doesn't sound right." The only requirements when praying are to believe He is listening to you and that He is willing to answer your requests (Hebrews 11:6).

"In this manner, therefore, pray: Our Father in heaven, Hallowed be Your name." (Mathew 6:9)

"And in that day you will ask Me nothing. Most assuredly, I say to you, whatever you ask the Father in My name He will give you." (John 16:23)

The Bible also shows us that we have been called to have fellowship with Jesus Christ (1 Corinthians 1:9); and with the Holy Spirit, who is our Guide, Comforter, and Teacher (John 16:13, 14:26). Throughout your day, you may talk to Jesus or to the Holy Spirit. Thank Him for His company, share with Him your plans, challenges, etc. Allow Him to guide you and comfort you through His Spirit.

WHEN FELLOWSHIP IS BROKEN

Who shall separate us from the love of Christ? Shall tribulation, or distress, or persecution, or famine, or nakedness, or peril, or sword? Yet in all these things we are more than conquerors through Him who loved us. For I am persuaded that neither death nor life, nor angels nor principalities nor powers, nor things present nor things to come, nor height nor depth, nor any other created thing, shall be able to separate us from the love of God which is in Christ Jesus our Lord. (Romans 8:35,37-39)

The Father's love is so wonderful. There is nothing that can separate you from it! By receiving this revelation in your life and deciding to trust Him, you are able to come boldly before Him without any fear.

Let us therefore come boldly to the throne of grace, that we may obtain mercy and find grace to help in time of need. (Hebrews 4:16)

Your new image as a new creation is based on the love of the Father toward you. As His child, you should never fear being rejected by Him. Neither should you fear disappointing Him, since He loved you and called you when you were in the worst condition you have ever been in.

But God, who is rich in mercy, because of His great love with which He loved us, even when we were dead in trespasses, made us alive together with Christ (by grace you have been saved). (Ephesians 2:4,5)

But what do we do when we fail His Word, and when we disobey and serve sin?

RELATIONSHIP AND FELLOWSHIP

In a family, when a child disobeys his father, it causes the communion or fellowship between them to be blocked. However, this disobedient action does not affect the relationship that exists between them, because their relationship is a result of a birthright, and not based on actions.

In the same way, we have relationship and fellowship with our heavenly Father.

- **Relationship.** Our relationship with the Father is based on the new birth. This relationship cannot be broken, since we are children of God through the blood of Jesus. And as His children, we no longer sin by nature (1 John 3:9). With the nature of God, we have power and freedom over sin.

- **Fellowship.** Our fellowship with the Father is based on the companionship that we have with Him, with His Word, and with our family in the faith (1 John 1:5,7). This fellowship can be broken through sinful actions.

RESTORING FELLOWSHIP

As new creations, we are a new spirit, pure and holy before God. However, our body and our mind need to be re-trained, or renewed, to our new life in Christ in order to change what the Bible calls the "old man," referring to the way that we used to think and act.

That you put off, concerning your former conduct, the old man which grows corrupt according to the deceitful lusts, and be renewed in the spirit of your mind, and that you put on the new man which was created according to God, in true righteousness and holiness. (Ephesians 4:22-24)

During this process of renewal, we will commit acts of disobedience and unbelief toward our Father and His Word. These actions of sin will hinder us from experiencing His fellowship and the guidance of His Spirit in our lives.

When this happens, the Father provides a way to restore fellowship with Him by confessing our sin and receiving His forgiveness by faith. When confessing your sin, you may say something like this, "Father, I confess that ____ (name what you did) is sin, and I ask forgiveness for it. Your Word says that by confessing my sin, you forgive me and cleanse me of it, and I thank you for that, in Jesus' name. Amen."

If we confess our sins, He is faithful and just to forgive us _our_ sins and to cleanse us from all unrighteousness. (1 John 1:9)

No matter how big your sin may seem, He promises to forgive you and forget your wrongdoing. Our Father is faithful and He is just!

Enjoy your fellowship with Him, and know that, if you sin, you can, in that same moment, confess your sin in an act of repentance and live free from condemnation.

There _is_ therefore now no condemnation to those who are in Christ Jesus, who do not walk according to the flesh, but according to the Spirit. (Romans 8:1)

Do not allow your mistakes from the past to rob you from enjoying the forgiveness and fellowship that the Father has provided you. Remember that your relationship with Him is not based on your works, but on His love for you. You are a child of God!

SELF QUIZ

As a new creation, how are you to relate to God?

Describe some characteristics of your heavenly Father, in contrast to your natural father.

Explain the difference between relationship and fellowship.

How is fellowship with the Father broken, and how is it restored?

5 BEING TRANSFORMED

Certainly, after learning of the truths about your new life and the love of the Father, you are ready to enjoy His fellowship and the freedom of redemption. To do this, you must continue with the process of renewing your mind.

During this study, you have received some information about the Word of God. And as you have believed and practiced the new information, it has not only fed you spiritually, but it has replaced wrong information you may have had in your mind regarding your identity as a child of God, about the Father, and about the Lord Jesus Christ.

This process of replacing the old way of thinking by applying the Word of God is known as the renewing of the mind.

FROM THOUGHT TO ACTION

For as he thinks in his heart, so is he. (Proverbs 23:7)

Every person, regardless of their position in Christ, experiences a process of thinking in their life which shapes their personality, attitudes, interests, behavior, emotional reactions, and character.

This process consists of a thought that turns into an action, which in turn becomes a habit, and finally a lifestyle. You are what you think!

CONFORMED TO THIS WORLD

And you He made alive, who were dead in trespasses and sins, in which you once walked according to the course of

this world, according to the prince of the power of the air, the spirit who now works in the sons of disobedience, among whom also we all once conducted ourselves in the lusts of our flesh, fulfilling the desires of the flesh and of the mind, and were by nature children of wrath, just as the others. (Ephesians 2:1-3)

If you have carefully read the previous verses, you will notice that the life that you lived before the new birth followed the course of the world, which is under the dominion of Satan. This type of life manifests itself in the desires of the flesh and in the thoughts.

Now, as a new creation, the Father exhorts you in His Word to no longer be conformed or molded to this world, but rather, to be transformed by the renewing of your mind.

And do not be conformed to this world, but be transformed by the renewing of your mind. (Romans 12:2)

TRANSFORMED

Remember that you are a spiritual being that lives in a body and operates through the mind. This spiritual being that you are, as we've seen previously, is pure and complete, ready to manifest the life of God in it.

Unfortunately, because of the natural world we live in, the only way to make evident the life of God that is in you, is through your soul and body, through a life of mental and physical prosperity.

How would you define mental and physical prosperity? Certainly, as a life free from fear and worries, a life full of joy and peace, with complete health and healing. And this is exactly what the Father desires for your soul and your body.

In fact, the Father desires that you reveal the quality of His life not only in your soul and body, but also in your social, financial, and familial areas. He desires your total prosperity!

Beloved, I pray that you may prosper in all things and be in health, just as your soul prospers. (3 John 2)

Perhaps you ask yourself, "If I am complete spiritually, why do I need to be transformed?" As we saw in the previous point, your mind and your body have been trained to think and act in the way that the world system operates. The way that the world operates leads to death through all that has to do with the nature of sin—fear, stress, selfishness, perversion, sickness, etc.

As a child of God, you must now re-train your mind and your body to think and act according to the ways of your new family, according to the Word of God. This way, the life that abides in you will be manifested in all your being, becoming a testimony to others.

Now may the God of peace Himself sanctify you completely; and may your whole spirit, soul, and body be preserved blameless at the coming of our Lord Jesus Christ. (1 Thessalonians 5:23)

In your new life, your responsibility is the transformation of your soul and your body through the renewing of your mind. This is an act of your will—a choice that *you* make.

THE WILL OF THE FATHER

And do not be conformed to this world, but be transformed by the renewing of your mind, that you may prove what *is* that good and acceptable and perfect will of God. (Romans 12:2)

Many Christians, due to a lack of knowledge of the Word of God and a mind that has not been renewed, believe that the will of God for their lives is a mystery. That it is something difficult to complete, or perhaps something that requires much sacrifice on their part.

But the Word shows us that by renewing our mind, we will not only be transformed in our soul and body, but we will also get to know the will of the Father for our lives, which is good, enjoyable, and perfect for each one of us.

RENEWING THE MIND

Before we were born again, we were spiritually dead. As a result, our walk depended totally on our five physical senses and our reasoning. As new creations, we are no longer limited to what we perceive with our senses; now we can be lead by the Spirit of our Father. We can now move beyond the natural. We can now move by faith.

In the process of renewing the mind, our goal is to train our mind to submit to God's Word, so that it can be an instrument of our spiritual being with which we will be able to interact with the natural world. Your mind, as well as your body, should be just that—instruments for the spirit, instead of being the parts that control your being.

And do not be conformed to this world, but be transformed by the renewing of your mind, that you may prove what is that good and acceptable and perfect will of God. (Romans 12:2)

The word "transformed" comes from the Greek word *metamorphoo*, which according to different dictionaries means:

- Physical or structural change
- Change of character, appearance or of condition

- Supernatural transformation due to supernatural powers
- Complete change of a person or thing

When your mind and body are transformed—conformed to the Word of God—you will be a new person not only spiritually, but physically as well!

Are you ready to learn more about how to renew your mind?

THE BATTLE IN THE MIND

For though we walk in the flesh, we do not war according to the flesh. For the weapons of our warfare are not carnal but mighty in God for pulling down strongholds, casting down arguments and every high thing that exalts itself against the knowledge of God, bringing every thought into captivity to the obedience of Christ. (2 Corinthians 10:3-5)

From the moment that you were born again, there has been a battle in your being. Your mind and your body are used to having control of your life, but now, your spirit is ready to take charge as it should. This battle for control causes conflict in your natural and mental parts.

You need to understand that your body and mind are not evil, even though at times they may seem to be your enemies— trying to stop you from walking in faith and obedience to the Word. They have simply been trained to act outside the Word in the natural realm. This is why we read that we are at war, but not against your flesh, or against other people.

The battle is in your mind, which has the power to control your body. Therefore, to win the battle, you need to gain control over your mind, through the powerful weapons that the Father has given you.

CONTROLLING YOUR THOUGHTS

Read again 2 Corinthians 10:3-5. You will realize that the battle primarily consists of destroying strongholds, demolishing arguments and any other haughtiness contrary to the knowledge of God, taking captive all thoughts, and submitting them to the obedience of Christ.

Are you ready to battle? Let's take time to study each one of these actions.

- **Destroying strongholds.** A stronghold is a fortified place that prevents what is inside from coming out, while at the same time, it prevents what is on the outside from coming in. The strongholds in your life are those thoughts of inability, inferiority, guilt, prejudices, and stereotypes that have created a great barrier in your mind. This barrier keeps you prisoner and at the same time it hinders new and different information from entering your mind.

  Therefore, to be free of this type of thinking, you need to destroy these strongholds through renewing your mind. You must exchange your existing thoughts that have kept you prisoner with new thoughts that are aligned to the Word of God.

- **Demolishing arguments.** Arguments are the logical thoughts or reasonings that hold you back from believing the spiritual and supernatural ways of God and His Word.

  When your mind doubts that the Father's promises will come to pass in your life, know that your mind has been trained to reason in this manner. But also know that your mind is capable of believing things that are not real according to the natural senses.

  For example, have you ever been afraid simply by hearing an old horror story? All of your five senses didn't experience such a story, however, in your imagination it was so real, that perhaps it caused your hands to sweat, or for you to react nervously. Let me give you another example. Imagine that you have a lemon in your hand. Imagine that while you are peeling it, that its juices are running through your fingers, and once peeled, you take a bite. Did your mouth water? Why? It wasn't real. It was simply in your mind, and in your imagination.

With this in mind, you are now aware that no matter how much your mind is used to reason and argue, it is also subject to believe things that are not real or that do not exist in the natural realm. Your mind, many times, cannot distinguish between what is real and not real. Therefore, if you train it to believe that the Word of God is real, eventually it will believe it, and you will win the battle of demolishing arguments.

- **Demolishing all haughtiness.** All haughtiness is every thought that lifts a barrier with the attitude of pride. These thoughts need to be demolished.

  In your Christian walk, you will find that many times the Word of God is going to correct you. Mainly when it teaches you that the manner in which you are acting or thinking is not correct according to the Word. Here is when you will have the opportunity to demolish the haughtiness in your mind by being submissive and teachable when receiving correction. Knowing that if the Father corrects you through His Word, it is because He loves you and wants your well-being (Hebrews 12:5-7).

- **Taking thoughts captive.** The Word exhorts us to take all thoughts captive to the obedience of Christ. It may sound complicated, but with practice and the knowledge of the Word of God, taking our thoughts captive becomes a lifestyle.

  To take thoughts captive means to determine if the thoughts that enter your mind agree with what the Word of God says. When they do not line up with the Word, then they must be replaced immediately.

Contrary to haughtiness, there is another extreme way of thinking—false humility. This attitude is as dangerous as pride. False humility refuses to receive the Father's promises and freedom, stating that we are not worthy of what God has made us worthy of. This is one of the thoughts that should be taken captive and replaced; otherwise, it will hinder our development and potential as children of God.

MIGHTY WEAPONS IN GOD

For the weapons of our warfare are not carnal but mighty in God. (2 Corinthians 10:4)

We have powerful weapons in God that give us the ability to destroy and take captive all thoughts contrary to the knowledge of God. What are these weapons?

And take the helmet of salvation, and the sword of the Spirit, which is the word of God. (Ephesians 6:17)

Ephesians 6:13-17 describes the different pieces that form the armor of God. This armor has been given to us so that we can win the battle in our mind.

Among the different pieces of this armor, you will find several defensive weapons and one offensive weapon. And although it is only one, this offensive weapon, the Word of God, is so powerful, that it is all that you need to be victorious in any battle.

Be diligent to present yourself approved to God, a worker who does not need to be ashamed, rightly dividing the word of truth. (2 Timothy 2:15)

Imagine a soldier in battle, protected by armor that envelopes him from head to toe, while wielding a powerful weapon against his enemy. Unless this soldier knows how to use his weapon, it becomes useless.

In the same manner, it is ineffective to posses in your hands the most powerful weapon—the Word of God—if you do not know how to use it. Let's see some ways in which we can benefit from this great weapon.

- **Listen** to God's Word. The first step to using the Word of God is to be taught. When hearing the Word, not only will you learn it, but it will also help to edify you and mature your faith.

  So then faith comes by hearing, and hearing by the word of God. (Romans 10:17)

- **Receive** God's Word. Once you've heard the Word, you must receive it. Recognize it as the highest authority in your life, with the attitude that you will submit to it and obey it.

  "But these are the ones sown on good ground, those who hear the word, accept it, and bear fruit: some thirtyfold, some sixty, and some a hundred." (Mark 4:20)

- **Meditate** on God's Word. To meditate on the Word is to remind yourself what you've been taught and to think on it. It is to imagine the Word becoming reality in your life, to study it, and to speak it in a soft voice to yourself.

  This Book of the Law shall not depart from your mouth, but you shall meditate in it day and night, that you may observe to do according to all that is written in it. For then you will make your way prosperous, and then you will have good success. (Joshua 1:8)

- **Act** on God's Word. When doing the Word, you show that you believe it, and as a doer of it, you will be blessed and prospered in whatever you do.

  But he who looks into the perfect law of liberty and continues in it, and is not a forgetful hearer but a doer of the work, this one will be blessed in what he does. (James 1:25)

- **Confess** God's Word. The Bible says that out of the abundance of the heart, the mouth speaks (Matthew 12:34). So when your thoughts, or your heart, is filled with the Word of God, you will begin to confess the Word without fear or shame, knowing that your Father is faithful to keep His promises.

  Let us hold fast the confession of our hope without wavering, for He who promised is faithful. (Hebrews 10:23)

- **Read** God's Word. Once you've heard the Word of God, you should study by yourself what you've been taught, having a dedicated time to read and review what you have learned.

  You search the Scriptures, for in them you think you have eternal life; and these are they which testify of Me. (John 5:39)

A LIVING SACRIFICE

I beseech you therefore, brethren, by the mercies of God, that you present your bodies a living sacrifice, holy, acceptable to God, which is your reasonable service. (Romans 12:1)

Notice that verse 1 of Romans 12 exhorts us to present our body as a living sacrifice, pleasing to God and holy, or set apart, to Him. How do we do this?

That you put off, concerning your former conduct, the old man which grows corrupt according to the deceitful lusts. (Ephesians 4:22)

Our body is a living sacrifice to God when, through a voluntary action, we take off the old man, with its old habits and traditions. Our bodies have been trained with deceitful desires. Desires that, although they may seem pleasant and beneficial, in reality they are painful and destructive.

Therefore, when your body desires to take part in or submit to an addiction, a bad habit, weakness, pain, or sickness, you need to meditate and confess what the Word of God says in regard to you and your body. Your body must submit to the Word of God. It doesn't have another option. To help it to obey, you can say something like this:

- "Body, you are a holy temple of the Spirit of God, and you have been separated exclusively for His use" (1 Corinthians 3:16)

- "Body, you have been freed from the authority and control of sin" (Romans 6:14)

- "I have been redeemed from the curse, therefore body, you have been redeemed from sickness and pain" (Galatians 3:13)

PUT ON THE NEW MAN

That you put off, concerning your former conduct, the old man which grows corrupt according to the deceitful lusts, and be renewed in the spirit of your mind, and that you put

on the new man which was created according to God, in true righteousness and holiness. (Ephesians 4:22-24)

Putting on the new man is to renew your mind according to the Word of God. This is your task and responsibility.

For laying aside the commandment of God, you hold the tradition of men … making the word of God of no effect through your tradition which you have handed down. (Mark 7:8,13)

From now on, you will need to make a decision. Will you hold on to your traditions? Your cultural, educational, and religious upbringing? Or, will you believe who God says you are, and what you can do, and have? When Christians live without renewing their mind, they literally void out the Word of God and leave it with no effect in their lives.

But we all, with unveiled face, beholding as in a mirror the glory of the Lord, are being transformed into the same image from glory to glory, just as by the Spirit of the Lord. (2 Corinthians 3:18)

Your life should be like a mirror of God's Word—revealing the image of Jesus Christ in you. Remember, the only way in which your life can be transformed to what the Father has designed for you is through renewing your mind.

Lastly, as you've noticed, to renew your mind you must know the Word of God. To help you in this area, toward the back of the book, you will find a section titled **"Think on These Things,"** which contains a list of Scriptures that will help you renew your mind regarding the different circumstances in your life.

SELF QUIZ

What part of your being must be transformed and why?

How are you transformed?

According to 2 Corinthians 10:3-5, how do we win the battle in the mind?

List six ways to use the Word of God.

6 OUR INHERITANCE AS CHILDREN

In our new family, the Father has not only made us His children, He has also made us His heirs!

And if children, then heirs–heirs of God and joint heirs with Christ. (Romans 8:17)

In our position as children, we do not need to beg the Father or try to convince Him in order to get His blessings. The moment we became part of His family, through the new birth, we became the legal heirs of all that He possesses.

JESUS CHRIST, HEIR OF ALL THINGS

"I will declare the decree: The LORD has said to Me, 'You are My Son, Today I have begotten You. Ask of Me, and I will give You The nations for Your inheritance, And the ends of the earth for Your possession. (Psalms 2:7,8)

Jesus Christ became the Father's heir through His victory over death and sin when He rose again from the dead. And when we received His redemptive work in our lives, we became one with Him. Consequently, through this union, we have become coheirs with Christ.

God, who at various times and in various ways spoke in time past to the fathers by the prophets, has in these last days spoken to us by *His* Son, whom He has appointed heir of all things, through whom also He made the worlds. (Hebrews 1:1,2)

This is wonderful news! As God's children, we can now enjoy the promises that the Father has prepared for His family.

Being part of our new family—the family of God—we have been given a new citizenship. In this new citizenship, we are governed under new laws and principles—the principles of the Kingdom of God.

All this sounds great, doesn't it? There is still more you need to know about your inheritance. Through the new birth, we became the righteousness of God in Christ (2 Corinthians 5:21). This righteousness not only gives us the legal right to come to the Father with boldness, without fear or guilt, it also gives us the legal right to appropriate our inheritance as children, as coheirs in Christ.

However, being children of God and being the righteousness of God in Christ does not guarantee that you enjoy your inheritance automatically. You must do something about it to be able to receive it and enjoy it.

In other words, even though your inheritance is available for you, here and now, the only way that you can enjoy it is by faith* and obedience to the principles of the Kingdom— through the renewing of your mind. Are you ready to enjoy your inheritance?

ENJOYING OUR INHERITANCE HERE AND NOW

Jesus answered, "Most assuredly, I say to you, unless one is born of water and the Spirit, he cannot enter the kingdom of God. (John 3:5)

Jesus said that by being born of the Spirit, we can enter the Kingdom of God. God's Kingdom is not only about heaven, as many have believed, but about living under God's reign, under His government, His principles, and His blessings.

The Father's desire is for you to live in an extraordinary way, taking advantage of the divine resources available for you, and having success in every area of your life.

Doing this will bring glory to the Father, because your life will be a representation of Him. Also, it will show the world the Father's love and kindness toward His own children, which will draw more people in to become part of His family (Romans 2:4).

For indeed, the kingdom of God is within you. (Luke 17:21)

One of Jesus' desires was for the Father's Kingdom to be manifested on earth in the same way that it is in heaven (Matthew 6:10).

That your days and the days of your children may be multiplied in the land of which the LORD swore to your fathers to give them, like the days of the heavens above the earth. (Deuteronomy 11:21)

Do you realize that God has determined His plan for your life, a plan of success and prosperity? You don't have to wait to be in heaven to enjoy it. Through His Word, you will receive direction as to how to appropriate the abundant life that belongs to you. Then, once you have received the Word's instruction, it is your responsibility to renew your mind, to believe what God says about who you are, what you can have, and what you can do.

Then it shall be to Me a name of joy, a praise, and an honor before all nations of the earth, who shall hear all the good that I do to them; they shall fear and tremble for all the goodness and all the prosperity that I provide for it. (Jeremiah 33:9)

Is it your desire to give joy and praise to your loving Father? Then start prospering. Enjoy your inheritance, and be a testimony to the nations! To receive and enjoy our inheritance is a personal decision that will introduce you to the best and the most satisfactory experience in your life.

EQUIPPED TO POSSESS

The Father has empowered you with all the necessary tools you need to obtain your inheritance. Before studying what our inheritance is all about, we will learn some useful tools that will help you to take possession of your inheritance.

- **Faith that moves mountains**

    When you were born again, you received the measure of faith that the Father gives to each one of His children. This measure of faith is the same for each Christian (2 Peter 1:1). The Bible compares it to a mustard seed that is able to produce abundant fruit (Matthew 17:20, 13:31,32).

    As God has dealt to each one a measure of faith. (Romans 12:3)

    Faith is believing and obeying the Word of God. We must do more than just believe it. In order to see the results of faith, we must *act* according to what the Word of God says. Acting on it is to obey it.

    For whatever is born of God overcomes the world. And this is the victory that has overcome the world— our faith. (1 John 5:4)

    The faith that you received from the Father has made you an overcomer!

- **Patience**

    Patience is an essential tool along with faith. Contrary to any negative definition we may have about this word, patience is a beautiful quality to possess.

And we desire that each one of you show the same
diligence to the full assurance of hope until the end,
that you do not become sluggish, but imitate those
who through faith and patience inherit the promises.
(Hebrews 6:11,12)

In the previous verses we see the way the Bible
defines patience. The Biblical meaning for patience is
not an attitude of inactivity, or the endurance of any
situation that comes against you, or a boring wait. No,
patience means to continue doing what you have
been doing. It means constancy and consistency. It is
to show the same diligence from the beginning until
the end.

Therefore do not cast away your confidence, which
has great reward. For you have need of endurance,
so that after you have done the will of God, you may
receive the promise. (Hebrews 10:35,36)

With the Holy Spirit within you, you have received the
seed of patience; this is a fruit that you must develop
in your life. The Father has equipped you with
patience—the ability to stay constant till the end!

• **Love**

The love that dwells in you is not an emotion or a
feeling; it is the Father's own nature in you. God is
love. Love is His nature (1 John 4:8).

Now hope does not disappoint, because the love of
God has been poured out in our hearts by the Holy
Spirit who was given to us. (Romans 5:5)

The love that the Father has poured in you is the
strength and the power that makes you a winner.
When you walk in His love, you cannot fail. The Word
says in 1 Corinthians 13:8 that love does not fail.

To walk in love is to keep the Word's commandments. It is to meditate on God's Word and to act on it (John 14:21).

The tool of love is also having an understanding of how much the Father loves you. As you get to know and receive the Father's love toward you, you will be perfected in love, and will be able to literally live a life free from fear.

There is no fear in love; but perfect love casts out fear, because fear involves torment. But he who fears has not been made perfect in love. (1 John 4:18)

• **Joy**

Joy is a tool that strengthens your life. Just as with faith, patience, and love, you have the Father's joy in you.

Do not sorrow, for the joy of the LORD is your strength. (Nehemiah 8:10)

To develop the joy of the Lord that will bring strength to your life, you don't need to rely on your feelings or your moods. To live in the joy of the Lord starts with a decision to renew your mind and meditate on the Father's love. Knowing that no matter what the situation you may be in, you have been predestined for victory. What a good reason to be joyful!

Rejoice always. (1 Thessalonians 5:16)

• **Many other tools**

Some other tools that the Father has given you, can be found in Galatians 5:22,23.

But the fruit of the Spirit is love, joy, peace, longsuffering, kindness, goodness, faithfulness, gentleness, self-control. Against such there is no law. (Galatians 5:22,23)

Use these tools available to you. The more you use them, the more you will master them. And know that "against such there is no law." In other words, these tools surpass natural laws, bringing you supernatural results.

THE PROMISED LAND

In the stories of the Old Testament, we see how God gave Israel a great land in which there was much prosperity and abundance. Once God established the inheritance for His people, it was up to them to go in and possess their promised land. In the same way, we as His people must go and possess our promised land.

For the LORD your God is bringing you into a good land, a land of brooks of water, of fountains and springs, that flow out of valleys and hills; a land of wheat and barley, of vines and fig trees and pomegranates, a land of olive oil and honey; a land in which you will eat bread without scarcity, in which you will lack nothing; a land whose stones are iron and out of whose hills you can dig copper. When you have eaten and are full, then you shall bless the LORD your God for the good land which He has given you. (Deuteronomy 8:7-10)

Now it is time to know what our inheritance consists of. Remember that to possess the promises mentioned later in this chapter, you must use your faith, believing that the Father has provided these promises for your possession. Believing that, as a child of God, you are a legal heir of what the Father has promised you. Have the attitude that these promises belong to you. Receive them by faith, and act on them. The natural manifestation will come.

Now faith is the substance of things hoped for, the evidence of things not seen. (Hebrews 11:1)

- **The Gift of the Spirit**

  As we saw previously, when we are born again, the Spirit of God comes to dwell in us, and we become one with Him. Unlike the indwelling of the Holy Spirit in your life, this is a gift that the Father has prepared for His children.

  This gift is to be filled or empowered with His Spirit. This empowerment happens when the Holy Spirit covers you with His power, giving you boldness to testify of Him (Acts 1:8).

  Receiving the gift of the Spirit, also gives you the ability to speak a new language—a spiritual language—which gives you the ability to pray to the Father when you don't know how to pray (Romans 8:26). Also, by using this spiritual language, you will build your own spirit and your faith. It will bring refreshment to your life, and it will assist you in receiving God's wisdom (1 Corinthians 14:4; Jude 20; 1 Corinthians 2:7,13).

  And they were all filled with the Holy Spirit and began to speak with other tongues, as the Spirit gave them utterance. (Acts 2:4)

- **Freedom from Fear**

  With the tool of love, we can live free from any fear (1 John 4:18).

  Inasmuch then as the children have partaken of flesh and blood, He Himself likewise shared in the same, that through death He might destroy him who had the power of death, that is, the devil, and release

those who through fear of death were all their lifetime subject to bondage. (Hebrews 2:14,15)

The Word says that the Father has not given you a spirit of fear, but of power, and of love, and of a sound mind (2 Timothy 1:7). Therefore, you should not live in fear. Fear will steal your joy, strength, health, and all that belongs to you. Fear is part of the devil's nature. His nature is to steal, to kill, and to destroy (John 10:10). Take possession of your inheritance and live free from fear!

Fear not, for I *am* with you; Be not dismayed, for I *am* your God. I will strengthen you, Yes, I will help you, I will uphold you with My righteous right hand. (Isaiah 41:10)

- **Health and Healing**

As children of God, we have been redeemed from the curse of sickness and death. The Word promises us long life filled with satisfaction (Psalm 91:16). No matter what the cause of sickness may be, we know that its source comes from the nature of death, and we are no longer partakers of that nature.

But He was wounded for our transgressions, He was bruised for our iniquities; The chastisement for our peace was upon Him, And by His stripes we are healed. (Isaiah 53:5)

On the cross, Jesus not only shed His blood for the forgiveness of our sins, but His body was also wounded and bruised in order to obtain our healing. There, He suffered all imaginable pain and sickness so that we don't have to suffer.

Your inheritance as a child of God is to receive your healing and restoration in every area of your soul and body that needs to be healed.

Once you have been healed and restored, your goal is to walk in complete health—divine health—taking authority over any symptom of illness that affects your body. Do not tolerate any sickness to dwell in your body. Health and healing belongs to you.

- **The Grace of God**

I thank my God always concerning you for the grace of God which was given to you by Christ Jesus, that you were enriched in everything by Him in all utterance and all knowledge, even as the testimony of Christ was confirmed in you, so that you come short in no gift, eagerly waiting for the revelation of our Lord Jesus Christ. (1 Corinthians 1:4-7)

God's grace can be defined in the following way: *Favor, delight, benefit, gift, reward, the sum of earthly blessings, abundance, liberality, power, and equipment for ministry, ability*, etc.

For now, we will refer to the grace of God as *the ability that He gives us to carry out any task*. This ability can be favor, creativity, finances, strength, etc.

The Word exhorts us to come before the Father with confidence knowing that, in Him, we will find whatever we need.

Let us therefore come boldly to the throne of grace, that we may obtain mercy and find grace to help in time of need. (Hebrews 4:16)

God's grace is also manifested in His love and mercy toward us by erasing all sins through the blood of Jesus. His grace to forgive is bigger than the biggest sin you could ever commit!

Moreover the law entered that the offense might abound. But where sin abounded, grace abounded much more. (Romans 5:20)

Do you need forgiveness, ability, favor, finances, etc.? They are all available to you. They are part of your inheritance, and you must possess them. Be a good steward of the manifold grace of God (1 Peter 4:10).

- **A New Beginning**

Do not remember the former things, Nor consider the things of old. Behold, I will do a new thing, Now it shall spring forth; Shall you not know it? I will even make a road in the wilderness *and* rivers in the desert. (Isaiah 43:18,19)

In Christ, we have the opportunity to start again, and again, and again, knowing that we can be forgiven and renewed as if we didn't have a past.

I, *even* I, *am* He who blots out your transgressions for My own sake; And I will not remember your sins. (Isaiah 43:25)

When we disobey or fail in walking in the Word of God, we know that the Father will give us another chance to start again. His desire is for us to get up and to keep on going. He is our best cheerleader!

We have already learned that when we confess our sins to the Father, He is faithful and just to forgive us and to cleanse us (1 John 1:9). Now, let's reinforce our security of a new beginning by being aware of our biggest obstacle when trying to start again after a fall—condemnation.

Condemnation and guilt are some of our enemy's favorite weapons against us. Before we were born again, he controlled and tortured us through them.

Even now, as new creations, the devil tries to use his same methods against us. Unfortunately, they keep working when a believer doesn't know that part of his inheritance is the privilege of a new beginning.

We also need to know the difference between temptation and sin, because many Christians are defeated by receiving condemnation when they are only being tempted.

Temptation, also known as *test* or *tribulation*, is not sin. The Bible tells us that Jesus was tempted in all forms (Hebrews 2:18, 4:15), but He never sinned. You are not guilty of sin when you are tempted. However, unless you take temptation captive by renewing your mind, temptation's seed will produce its fruit, which is sin.

Let no one say when he is tempted, "I am tempted by God"; for God cannot be tempted by evil, nor does He Himself tempt anyone. But each one is tempted when he is drawn away by his own desires and enticed. Then, when desire has conceived, it gives birth to sin; and sin, when it is full-grown, brings forth death. (James 1:13-15)

Remember that your enemy, the devil, is a thief, a destroyer, and a murderer. He wants to steal your freedom as a child of God, and he wants to destroy your future through sin that produces death.

Your inheritance in God is a secure and prosperous future, a life full of success. Take possession of this inheritance and keep pressing on, starting over again, if it is necessary. Know that there is no condemnation for those who are in Christ (Romans 8:1).

Brethren, I do not count myself to have apprehended; but one thing *I do*, forgetting those things which are behind and reaching forward to

those things which are ahead, I press toward the goal for the prize of the upward call of God in Christ Jesus. (Philippians 3:13,14)

- **Prosperity**

And you shall remember the LORD your God, for *it is* He who gives you power to get wealth, that He may establish His covenant which He swore to your fathers, as *it is* this day. (Deuteronomy 8:18)

We have been created to have all of our needs provided for, and even exceedingly met. Before sin entered the world, working was not a means of survival. God assigned work to Adam as a way to govern and take care of His creation.

In the Bible, we find numerous verses affirming the Father's desire to prosper us in every area, including financially. But our astute enemy has tried to twist the Word of God through religion in order for us to believe that the purest way to serve God is through poverty and misery. This is a big lie!

We can see from the Old to the New Testament, that each person who walked in close fellowship with God and kept His commandments had their needs provided for and received prosperity and financial abundance. At the beginning of the story, in Genesis, we see that Adam and Eve had all their needs provided for. When we see the end of the story, in Revelation, with a new sky and a new earth, we again find abundance.

Poverty and lack are not included in God's plan for His creation. It was through sin that the curse entered earth, and poverty is part of the curse.

For you know the grace of our Lord Jesus Christ, that though He was rich, yet for your sakes He became poor, that you through His poverty might become rich. (2 Corinthians 8:9)

When Jesus Christ came to the world, He lived a prosperous life. At the cross He took the curse upon Himself. He took all our poverty and lack, so that we can be partakers of His riches—material riches.

Living financially prosperous is the best way in which we will be able to take care of our Father's business— serving Him and being a testimony to the world, showing people that our Father is the God of the whole earth, and that we are His heirs.

THE PEOPLE OF GOD

There are so many other promises that are part of our inheritance in God. We have been promised victory, protection, favor, the service of angels, spiritual gifts, divine wisdom, etc.

For now, you can use the promises mentioned before to meditate on and to renew your mind.

Recognize that, as a child and heir of God, you cannot see yourself the way that you used to. Your identity has changed; your future has changed. You are no longer the same person; you are a new creation. You belong to a new family; therefore, you must practice new principles, new habits, and speak new words. You are not the same; you are a child of God. Live as a child of God!

But you *are* a chosen generation, a royal priesthood, a holy nation, His own special people, that you may proclaim the praises of Him who called you out of darkness into His marvelous light. (1 Peter 2:9)

SELF QUIZ

Who are you according to Romans 8:17?

When and where are you supposed to enjoy your inheritance?

List three tools you must use to receive your inheritance.

List four areas that are part of your inheritance as a child of God.

7 GOD'S FAMILY

Now, therefore, you are no longer strangers and foreigners, but fellow citizens with the saints and members of the household of God. (Ephesians 2:19)

As a child of God, you are now part of the family of faith, the family of God. In this family, as well as in a natural family, you have a place and a special function. For you to be completely fulfilled in life, you must live knowing and experiencing the Father's love and promises for you. You must also live knowing and fulfilling your purpose in your new family.

Therefore, as we have opportunity, let us do good to all, especially to those who are of the household of faith. (Galatians 6:10)

In the previous verse, God exhorts us to do good and be a blessing to all, but especially to the family of faith.

In this chapter, we will study about God's family and the way for you to be a blessing in it. We will begin with looking at some of the functions that Jesus had here on earth, and His current position in the family of faith. As first-born in this family, He has established for us the example to follow.

JESUS' MINISTRY ON EARTH

God's Word shows us some specific functions that Jesus Christ fulfilled here on earth. Through the Gospels, we can see that one of Jesus' main functions was to reveal the Father.

Contrary to the image that religion had established about God, Jesus devoted Himself to show people the Father's heart toward humanity, and His desire for restoration through forgiveness of sin, healing, deliverance, and provision. Jesus, through His words and actions, showed the world that the heavenly Father loves and cares for His creation (John 14:6,7; Colossians 1:15; Hebrews 1:3).

In addition to revealing the Father, Jesus came:
- To destroy the works of the devil (1 John 3:8)
- To complete the Father's will (John 6:38)
- To show men the way to the Father (John 14:6)
- To preach the Kingdom of God and testify of the truth (Luke 4:43; John 18:37)
- To serve, and to give His life as a ransom for many (Matthew 20:28)

JESUS AND THE CHURCH

And I also say to you that you are Peter, and on this rock I will build My church, and the gates of Hades shall not prevail against it. (Matthew 16:18)

After completing His ministry on earth, Jesus Christ showed His next priority and current ministry—God's family, also known as the Church.

When the Word of God mentions the Church, it talks about either God's universal family—believers around the world—or a group of believers that gather in a specific place, also known as the local church.

Let's see in the following verse Jesus' love and purpose toward His church.

Just as Christ also loved the church and gave Himself for her, that He might sanctify and cleanse her with the washing of water by the word, that He might present her to Himself a glorious church, not having spot or wrinkle or any such thing, but that she should be holy and without blemish. (Ephesians 5:25-27)

Can you see it? Just as Jesus loves you individually and desires you to live in complete abundance (John 10:10), in the same way, He desires that corporately, as a family, Christians live in a glorious way. His family—His church, is a glorious church!

THE BODY OF CHRIST

Once Jesus completed His ministry on earth and ascended back to heaven, God the Father seated Him at His right hand in heavenly places, and gave Him authority and dominion over all things, in all places, for all eternity (Ephesians 1:20-23).

And He put all *things* under His feet, and gave Him *to be* head over all *things* to the church. (Ephesians 1:22)

Jesus Christ governs over the Church. He is its head (Colossians 1:18). The Church is Christ's body through which He speaks and acts. The Church is the means by which He can fill all places with His presence!

As you can see, the Church is Jesus Christ's primary focus because it is the way in which He operates now on earth. As part of the family of God, you are part of the church. You are part of the body of Christ!

For as we have many members in one body, but all the members do not have the same function. (Romans 12:4)

YOUR PLACE IN THE BODY

The moment you were born again, God the Father placed you in the body of Christ. Likewise, as each member of the human body is important, you are a very important and necessary part of the body of Christ.

For as the body is one and has many members, but all the members of that one body, being many, are one body, so also *is* Christ. For by one Spirit we were all baptized into one body—whether Jews or Greeks, whether slaves or free—and have all been made to drink into one Spirit. For in fact the body is not one member but many. But now God has set the members, each one of them, in the body just as He pleased. And if they *were* all one member, where *would* the body *be?* But now indeed *there are* many members, yet one body. Now you are the body of Christ, and members individually. (1 Corinthians 12:12-14, 18-20, 27)

In the same way that Jesus fulfilled different functions while being on earth, you, as part of His body, have specific functions to fulfill. Just as Jesus did, you have a ministry to accomplish.

Next, we will study what this ministry is all about, and how to receive the necessary training to carry it out.

GOD'S CALLING IN YOUR LIFE

For whom He foreknew, He also predestined *to be* conformed to the image of His Son, that He might be the firstborn among many brethren. Moreover whom He predestined, these He also called; whom He called, these He also justified; and whom He justified, these He also glorified. (Romans 8:29-30)

You have been called by God to partake of the blessings of redemption (2 Timothy 1:9). This call also includes assuming a certain title or vocation. The previous verse shows us that God has called us to be conformed to the image of His Son.

Being called by God, you must live in a way that reflects the image of the Son to people around you. This is why we previously mentioned some functions or characteristics of Jesus' walk in this world. Knowing the way Jesus operated here on earth, you will be able to follow His example, and as a result, you will fulfill your calling.

Therefore, brethren, be even more diligent to make your call and election sure, for if you do these things you will never stumble. (2 Peter 1:10)

God the Father loves us so much, that anytime He commands us to do something, it is always for our benefit. The previous verse gives us a wonderful promise for our success. It tells us that when we are diligent in our call, we will be delivered from failure!

Let's see some of the functions that we can carry out to complete this calling.

GREATER WORKS

While on earth, Jesus Christ performed great miracles and wonders, transforming many lives by ministering love, truth, hope, comfort, freedom, and so much more.

Let's review some functions of Jesus' ministry on earth, which you will be able to continue while fulfilling your calling:

- To reveal the Father
- To destroy the works of the devil
- To complete the Father's will
- To show men the way to the Father
- To preach the Kingdom of God (God's way of doing things)
- To give testimony of the truth
- To serve

Most assuredly, I say to you, he who believes in Me, the works that I do he will do also; and greater *works* than these he will do, because I go to My Father. (John 14:12)

Jesus Christ told His disciples—including you and me—that once we are born-again believers, we can continue doing the works that He did and even greater ones.

Can you see yourself doing these works and even greater ones? If your answer at the moment is "no," it's okay. Your role for now is to mature and to receive more instruction. To help change any negative images you may have about yourself, you must go through a process of maturation by receiving instruction. Then you will be able to see yourself with the ability in Christ to do His works and even greater ones.

If you remember, at the beginning of the book, we explained that a baby, as a new member in a family, is in the position to only receive unconditional love, security, protection, and provision. As he matures, he will eventually learn his own position, and the positions of the other members of the family. Through time, he will receive specific responsibilities that will benefit his own well-being as well as that of his family.

In your new family, your heavenly Father does not expect you to do something without the necessary maturity. However, you must know that you already have all the capacity that you need to complete the whole purpose of God in your life. Just as a newborn baby has the necessary members in his body to walk, and even to run, he doesn't have the maturity to do it.

In the same way, the moment you were born again, you received all ability to carry out the call of God on your life. Prior to handling this, it is necessary that you grow and mature in your new identity as a new creation, in the Father's love toward you, in the security in your redemption, and in your rights and privileges as a child of God.

Having a good foundation in this truth will give you the maturity to fulfill God's calling on your life, and the ability to bless the family of the faith, the world around you, as well as yourself.

THE IMPORTANCE OF THE CHURCH

As a child of God, you are already part of the universal family of God. However, to be able to grow and mature in your new identity, you need to be part of a local family of faith—a local church.

The Word of God shows us that through history, the way God has organized and dealt with His people has been through groups of people guided by a leader. In the New Testament, every instruction and blessing to born-again believers was communicated to the local churches through a leader or pastor.

Then those who gladly received his word were baptized; and that day about three thousand souls were added *to them.* And they continued steadfastly in the apostles' doctrine and fellowship, in the breaking of bread, and in prayers. (Acts 2:41-42)

Once Jesus ascended back to heaven, the Church was instituted through local gatherings with the purpose of maturing and equipping believers in their new life.

In the previous verse, we find some key elements in which these gatherings consisted of: the apostles' instructions, fellowship with other believers, breaking of bread, and prayer.

As you can see, the church is a major place to mature in your new identity. Pray to the Father to help you find a church where God's Word and Jesus Christ as Lord and Savior are preached. In the right church, you will find the same characteristics of the church mentioned in Acts 2:42:

- Teaching of the Word of God, including the message of salvation through the redemptive work of Jesus Christ
- Fraternal fellowship

- Breaking of bread for fellowship's sake, and in remembrance of Jesus' sacrifice for us, as well as to proclaim His coming
- Teaching and practice of prayer

A PASTOR–JESUS' GIFT TO YOU

And I will give you shepherds according to My heart, who will feed you with knowledge and understanding. (Jeremiah 3:15)

Just as in a family there is a leader (in general, it is the father), in the church's family, God has provided a spiritual father or shepherd. This shepherd's role is to feed you the Word of God, and guide you in your Christian walk through exhortation, instruction, and correction (2 Timothy 3:16).

I will set up shepherds over them who will feed them; and they shall fear no more, nor be dismayed, nor shall they be lacking," says the Lord. (Jeremiah 23:4)

Being part of a local church and having a pastor in your life gives you the opportunity to receive the benefits listed in the previous verse. Being fed biblically for your growth and maturity will enable you to live a life free from fear, free from failure, and free from lack.

YOUR FUNCTION IN THE LOCAL CHURCH

And He Himself gave some *to be* apostles, some prophets, some evangelists, and some pastors and teachers, for the equipping of the saints for the work of ministry, for the edifying of the body of Christ, till we all come to the unity of the faith and of the knowledge of the Son of God, to a perfect man, to the measure of the stature of the fullness of Christ; that we should no longer be children, tossed to and fro and carried about with every wind of doctrine, by the trickery of men, in the cunning craftiness of deceitful plotting, but, speaking the truth in love, may grow up in all things into Him who is the head–Christ—from whom the whole body, joined and knit together by what every joint supplies, according to the effective working by which every part does its share, causes growth of the body for the edifying of itself in love. (Ephesians 4:11-16)

Remember that God has instituted the local church as a place where you will be part of a family with the same faith, in which you will be able to develop into the person that He designed and destined you to be.

In this family of faith, in addition to receiving spiritual food and protection, you can be matured and trained in your calling to be conformed to the image of the Son.

Simultaneously, it will provide you a perfect opportunity to carry out the ministry of Jesus in your surroundings, and fulfill the ordinance of Galatians 6:10 to be a blessing, especially to the family of faith.

And let us consider one another in order to stir up love and good works, not forsaking the assembling of ourselves together, as *is* the manner of some, but exhorting *one another,* and so much the more as you see the Day approaching. (Hebrews 10:24-25)

Once incorporated in a local church, be faithful with your attendance. Obey the pastor and the teachings of the Word by putting what you learn into practice in your life.

Make a commitment regarding your attendance, time, financial resources, and possess a positive attitude. Participating in the different ministries in your church will help you become familiar with your new church family more quickly. Be considerate and patient in learning about the church.

Do not allow trivial things such as uneasiness, lack of knowledge, preconceived ideas, or misunderstandings hinder your growth in the church. Or even worse, create an offense in your life against the church. Remember that bad experiences can happen even in the best of families! The local church is a family of believers with different levels of maturity, each one growing in their new identity, and corporally becoming a glorious church.

CONCLUSION

Therefore we also pray always for you that our God would count you worthy of *this* calling, and fulfill all the good pleasure of *His* goodness and the work of faith with power, that the name of our Lord Jesus Christ may be glorified in you, and you in Him, according to the grace of our God and the Lord Jesus Christ. (2 Thessalonians 1:11-12)

An exciting life awaits you by being established in your new identity as a child of God! Knowing the benefits of redemption, growing in the Father's love and fellowship, renewing your mind with the Word of God, and partaking of your inheritance, will all equip and empower you to venture out into fulfilling your God-given purpose in life.

Do not be discouraged when circumstances are not the way you expected them to be. Use the tools of faith the Father has given you and let Him manifest Himself greatly in your life.

You are a child of God. My prayer is for you to live as one. May your life be a testimony of the Father's wonderful love, and what Jesus Christ obtained for you when He became the Lord of lords and King of kings!

SELF QUIZ

What are the main features of a Biblical church according to Acts 2:41,42?

What is God's call on your life, according to Romans 8:29,30?

List seven functions with which you can continue Jesus' ministry on earth.

List three of God's promises made available to you by having a pastor in your life.

What is your function in the local church?

Describe the way your identity in Christ has changed after reading this book.

THINK ON THESE THINGS...

Finally, brethren, whatever things are true, whatever things *are* noble, whatever things *are* just, whatever things *are* pure, whatever things *are* lovely, whatever things *are* of good report, if *there is* any virtue and if *there is* anything praiseworthy—meditate on these things. (Philippians 4:8)

The following are some Biblical verses that will help you to renew your mind. When you deal with any of the following issues, take control of any thought contrary to the Word, by confessing and meditating on what the Father has declared and promised in your life.

The more you practice confessing and meditating on these Scriptures, you will notice your thoughts eventually coming in line with the Father's thoughts according to His Word. This will help facilitate living in and enjoying your new identity in Christ. Lastly, keep in mind that the process of renewing your mind is a daily task, and a lifelong practice.

WHAT GOD'S WORD SAYS ABOUT...

• **My Salvation**

For God so loved the world that He gave His only begotten Son, that whoever believes in Him should not perish but have everlasting life. For God did not send His Son into the world to condemn the world, but that the world through Him might be saved. (John 3:16,17)

For by grace you have been saved through faith, and that not of yourselves; *it is* the gift of God, not of works, lest anyone should boast. (Ephesians 2:8,9)

That if you confess with your mouth the Lord Jesus and believe in your heart that God has raised Him from the dead, you will be saved. For with the heart one believes unto righteousness, and with the mouth confession is made unto salvation. (Romans 10:9,10)

But as many as received Him, to them He gave the right to become children of God, to those who believe in His name. (John 1:12)

Not by works of righteousness which we have done, but according to His mercy He saved us, through the washing of regeneration and renewing of the Holy Spirit. (Titus 3:5)

- **Forgiveness of Sins**

    Therefore, if anyone *is* in Christ, *he is* a new creation; old things have passed away; behold, all things have become new. (2 Corinthians 5:17)

    If we confess our sins, He is faithful and just to forgive us *our* sins and to cleanse us from all unrighteousness. (1 John 1:9)

    To Him all the prophets witness that, through His name, whoever believes in Him will receive remission of sins. (Acts 10:43)

    In whom we have redemption through His blood, the forgiveness of sins. (Colossians 1:14)

    Who forgives all your iniquities, Who heals all your diseases. (Psalms 103:3)

- **My Future**

    For I know the thoughts that I think toward you, says the Lord, thoughts of peace and not of evil, to give you a future and a hope. (Jeremiah 29:11)

This Book of the Law shall not depart from your mouth, but you shall meditate in it day and night, that you may observe to do according to all that is written in it. For then you will make your way prosperous, and then you will have good success. (Joshua 1:8)

Trust in the Lord with all your heart, And lean not on your own understanding; In all your ways acknowledge Him, And He shall direct your paths. (Proverbs 3:5,6)

But the path of the just *is* like the shining sun, That shines ever brighter unto the perfect day. (Proverbs 4:18)

The Lord will open to you His good treasure, the heavens, to give the rain to your land in its season, and to bless all the work of your hand. You shall lend to many nations, but you shall not borrow. (Deuteronomy 28:12)

- **My Health**

Beloved, I pray that you may prosper in all things and be in health, just as your soul prospers. (3 John 1:2)

Surely He has borne our griefs And carried our sorrows; Yet we esteemed Him stricken, Smitten by God, and afflicted. But He *was* wounded for our transgressions, *He was* bruised for our iniquities; The chastisement for our peace *was* upon Him, And by His stripes we are healed. (Isaiah 53:4,5)

Who forgives all your iniquities, Who heals all your diseases. (Psalms 103:3)

He sent His word and healed them, And delivered *them* from their destructions. (Psalms 107:20)

Is anyone among you sick? Let him call for the elders of the church, and let them pray over him, anointing him with oil in the name of the Lord. And the prayer of faith will save the sick, and the Lord will raise him up. And if he has committed sins, he will be forgiven. (James 5:14,15)

- **My Mental Peace**

  You will keep *him* in perfect peace, *Whose* mind *is* stayed *on You,* Because he trusts in You. (Isaiah 26:3)

  Be anxious for nothing, but in everything by prayer and supplication, with thanksgiving, let your requests be made known to God; and the peace of God, which surpasses all understanding, will guard your hearts and minds through Christ Jesus. (Philippians 4:6,7)

  And let the peace of God rule in your hearts, to which also you were called in one body; and be thankful. (Colossians 3:15)

  For God has not given us a spirit of fear, but of power and of love and of a sound mind. (2 Timothy 1:7)

  There is no fear in love; but perfect love casts out fear, because fear involves torment. But he who fears has not been made perfect in love. (1 John 4:18)

- **My Finances**

  And you shall remember the Lord your God, for *it is* He who gives you power to get wealth, that He may establish His covenant which He swore to your fathers, as *it is* this day. (Deuteronomy 8:18)

  Honor the Lord with your possessions, And with the firstfruits of all your increase; So your barns will be filled with plenty, And your vats will overflow with new wine. (Proverbs 3:9,10)

  Beloved, I pray that you may prosper in all things and be in health, just as your soul prospers. (3 John 1:2)

  But this *I say:* He who sows sparingly will also reap sparingly, and he who sows bountifully will also reap bountifully. So let each one *give* as he purposes in his heart, not grudgingly or of necessity; for God loves a cheerful giver. And God *is* able to make all grace abound toward you, that you, always having all sufficiency in all *things,* may have an abundance for every good work... while *you are* enriched in everything for all liberality, which causes thanksgiving through us to God. (2 Corinthians 9:6-8,11)

The Lord *is* my shepherd; I shall not want. (Psalms 23:1)

- **My Prayers**

And whatever you ask in My name, that I will do, that the Father may be glorified in the Son. If you ask anything in My name, I will do *it.* (John 14:13,14)

If you abide in Me, and My words abide in you, you will ask what you desire, and it shall be done for you. (John 15:7)

Be anxious for nothing, but in everything by prayer and supplication, with thanksgiving, let your requests be made known to God. (Philippians 4:6)

The Lord *is* far from the wicked, But He hears the prayer of the righteous. (Proverbs 15:29)

Beloved, if our heart does not condemn us, we have confidence toward God. And whatever we ask we receive from Him, because we keep His commandments and do those things that are pleasing in His sight. (1 John 3:21,22)

- **My Words**

Death and life *are* in the power of the tongue, And those who love it will eat its fruit. (Proverbs 18:21)

Let your speech always *be* with grace, seasoned with salt, that you may know how you ought to answer each one. (Colossians 4:6)

A soft answer turns away wrath, But a harsh word stirs up anger. (Proverbs 15:1)

If anyone speaks, *let him speak* as the oracles of God. If anyone ministers, *let him do it* as with the ability which God supplies, that in all things God may be glorified through Jesus Christ, to whom belong the glory and the dominion forever and ever. Amen. (1 Peter 4:11)

Therefore, putting away lying, "*Let* each one *of you* speak truth with his neighbor," for we are members of one another. (Ephesians 4:25)

- **My Protection**

The name of the Lord *is* a strong tower; The righteous run to it and are safe. (Proverbs 18:10)

Because you have made the Lord, *who is* my refuge, *Even* the Most High, your dwelling place, No evil shall befall you, Nor shall any plague come near your dwelling; For He shall give His angels charge over you, To keep you in all your ways. (Psalms 91:9-11)

The angel of the Lord encamps all around those who fear Him, And delivers them. (Psalms 34:7)

The Lord *is* near to those who have a broken heart, And saves such as have a contrite spirit. (Psalms 34:18)

In righteousness you shall be established; You shall be far from oppression, for you shall not fear; And from terror, for it shall not come near you... No weapon formed against you shall prosper, And every tongue *which* rises against you in judgment You shall condemn. This *is* the heritage of the servants of the Lord, And their righteousness *is* from Me," Says the Lord. (Isaiah 54:14,17)

How to receive Jesus Christ
as your Lord and Savior

The Bible says, "That if you confess with your mouth the Lord Jesus and believe in your heart that God has raised Him from the dead, you will be saved. For with the heart one believes unto righteousness, and with the mouth confession is made unto salvation." (Romans 10:9,10)

To receive Jesus Christ as your Lord and Savior, you may pray a prayer like this, believing with your heart and confessing with your mouth:

> *Lord Jesus,*
> *I believe you came to earth to die on the cross for me, and that you rose again on the third day. Thank you for loving me and giving me the opportunity of a new life in You. This day I confess You as the Lord and Savior of my life. And I thank you that now I am saved!*

If you just received Jesus as your Lord and Savior, then congratulations and welcome to God's family! Today you have been born again and became a child of God. Remember this special date and keep moving forward in your new walk in Christ.

Made in the USA
Las Vegas, NV
15 February 2021